42 × 29.7　Pencil Watercolor Pastel Colored pencil, Kent paper

54.7 × 39.5   Pencil Watercolor Pastel, Kent paper

42×29.7 Pencil, Skin paper

27.5×29.5   *Pencil, Skin paper*

2

42 × 29.7   Pencil, Skin paper

FIGURE DRAWING
FOR FASHION

Copyright© 1986 Graphic-sha Publishing Co., Ltd.
1-9-12 Kudankita, Chiyoda-ku, Tokyo 102, Japan.
ISBN 4-7661-0389-0

Printed in Japan

First Printing, 1986

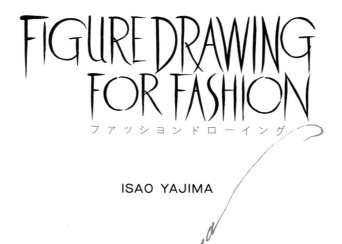

FIGURE DRAWING FOR FASHION

ファッションドローイング

ISAO YAJIMA

g

GRAPHIC-SHA

■凡例

それぞれの作品には、サイズ (センチ)、画材 (Pencil：ペンシル、Colored pencil：カラーペンシル、Conte：コンテ、Pastel：パステル、Marker：マーカー、Gouache：グワッシュ、Watercolor：水彩、Airbrush：エアブラシ)、紙の種類 (Watercolor paper：水彩紙、Kent paper：ケント紙、BB Kent paper：BBケント紙、Skin paper：スキンペーパー、Fabriano paper：ファブリアーノ紙、Mat paper：ニューエイジ紙、Drawing paper：上質紙、PM pad：PM パッド紙) を表記しています。

CONTENTS

PROLOGUE········· 1

TITLE········· 7

PENCIL········· 1, 2, 3, 23, 32, 35, 40, 41, 46, 50, 51, 54–58, 63, 65, 67, 84, 86, 88, 89, 92, 104, 105, 117

PENCIL & CHINESE INK········· 20–22

PENCIL & COLORED PENCIL········· 38, 39

PENCIL, CHINESE INK & GOUACHE········· 83

PENCIL & PASTEL········· 15–17, 26, 27, 30, 31, 44, 45, 60, 61, 90, 91, 99, 114, 116, 124

PENCIL, PASTEL & COLORED PENCIL········· 94–97

PENCIL, PASTEL & WATERCOLOR········· 103, 105–108, 110, 111, 115

PENCIL, PASTEL & AIRBRUSH········· 34

PENCIL & CONTE········· 28, 29

PENCIL & WATERCOLOR········· 33, 40, 42, 59, 64, 78, 79, 81, 83, 102, 112, 126, 127

PENCIL, WATERCOLOR & MARKER········· 43

PENCIL, WATERCOLOR & COLORED PENCIL········· 82, 87

PENCIL, WATERCOLOR & PASTEL········· 83

PENCIL, WATERCOLOR, PASTEL & CONTE········· 93

PENCIL & GOUACHE········· 22, 36, 37, 47–57, 59, 62, 66–77, 80, 82, 83, 91, 120, 121

PENCIL, GOUACHE & PASTEL········· 78, 82, 119

PENCIL, GOUACHE & COLORED PENCIL········· 85

CONTE PENCIL & PASTEL········· 98

CONTE PENCIL, WATERCOLOR & COLORED PENCIL········· 100

CONTE PENCIL & COLORED PENCIL········· 101

「イラストは目で見るファッショントーキング。時にはフォトより雄弁に、そして暖かく私達に話しかける。矢島功の画にはポエムがある。現代のモードを代弁する詩がある。」

Illustration is fashion talking to us visually. Often it speaks with more eloquence and warmth than photography. Isao Yajima's illustrations are poems. They speak in the mode of the day.

(Hair Artist)

近 江 禮 一 （ヘアーアーティスト）
Reiichi Ohmi

矢島功は名人である。イラストレーションのクラシズムを、迷いなく、シャープに、風のように指先が切り取ってしまう名人。名人達をはしる俗人達の一人。「イラップに矢島功」

Isao Yajima is a master. Without a doubt he is a master sprinting ahead in the classicism of illustration. Like the wind his fingertips sharply carve out the genre.

(Mode Designer)

山 本 耀 司 （モードデザイナー）
Yohji Yamamoto

矢島氏　とは旧知の仲であるが、お会いするたびに感じることがある。
彼の作品が独特の素晴しい世界を持っているのは勿論だが、彼にはこの作風プラス α（ア
ルファ）があるように思えるのだ。そのプラス αとは、イラストレーターが持つ「絵」と
いう空間だけではなく、「他の行動方法でも自からを表現したい」という渇望ではないか
と思う。それは何か別の形のクリエーションであるのか、もっと、とてつもないことかは
わからないが。

Yajima and I have been friends for a long time now, and whenever I meet him I
am always impressed. Certainly, his work is unique and is a wonderful world of
its own. Yet I feel that there is also something extra —— his style plus alpha.
This alpha is not just the space of the illustrator's "picture", I think it is his craving
to express himself in another dynamic way. Whether it is another form of creation
or something more way out, I will not be able to make imagination about it.

(Mode Designer)

や ま も と　寛 斎　（モードデザイナー）
Kansai Yamamoto

わが同級生の中で、いちばん才能が開花したのは、矢島功氏である。軽いフットワークで、イラストレーションの世界に叙情性を昇華させるのだ。

Of all the students in our class Isao Yajima was the one whose talent really bloomed. With his light footwork he actually sublimates lyricism in the world of illustration.

(Chief Editor of 25ans magazine)

戸田麒一郎　（ヴァンサンカン編集長）
Kiichiro Toda

はじめに

ファッション画を描くとき、私はどのような手順で描い
ているのかあまり秩序立てて考えたことがありません。
前もって、こう仕上げようと考えたものも、途中で必ず
予期していなかったことに出合います。
画材も描く上で決められた約束ごとは何ひとつありませ
ん。技術といっても、実際は画材と慣れ親しんでいくう
ちに、その時々の偶然がもたらす思いがけない表情がつ
み重なって、アイデアに結びついていきます。
スティリストから提示された服の中には、必ず表現して
ほしい部分があります。そのイメージを捉えるまでに、
一番時間がかかります。しかし、そのこと以外は自由に
描けるわけです。
ファッションは、日常的で楽しい遊びの中にあると思い
ます。服も同じで、自由な部分をそうした自分なりに遊
びで創り変えてしまいます。
つまり、私にとって画を描くことも日常の遊びのひとつ
なのだと思います。

FOREWORD

When beginning a fashion drawing, It rarely happens that
I have organized which to start with first. Even if I have
a preconceived idea of how it is going to work out,
something unexpected is sure to crop up in the process.
Even as for the medium I am going to use, I don't admit
what they should be applied when drawing. I could say
there's a technique, but in actual fact, as I proceed and get
the feel of my medium, the unexpected sometimes
happens and I express something that I hadn't even plan-
ned. These unexpected expressions accumulate and
become a part of the overall idea.
In the clothes presented by a stylist there is always an
element in which he wants to express himself. This is the
hardest part to catch in an illustration. Apart from this
part, I draw freely as it comes.
To me, fashion is fun; it is a part of everyday play. I
think it can be said with clothes, too. And in the same
way, drawing is to me just another part of everyday play.

放物線を描いていると、女性の体に見えてくる。大小さまざまな
うねりの線、それに、ジグザグは質量の運動を表わし、点線は、
それらの残像をイメージする。

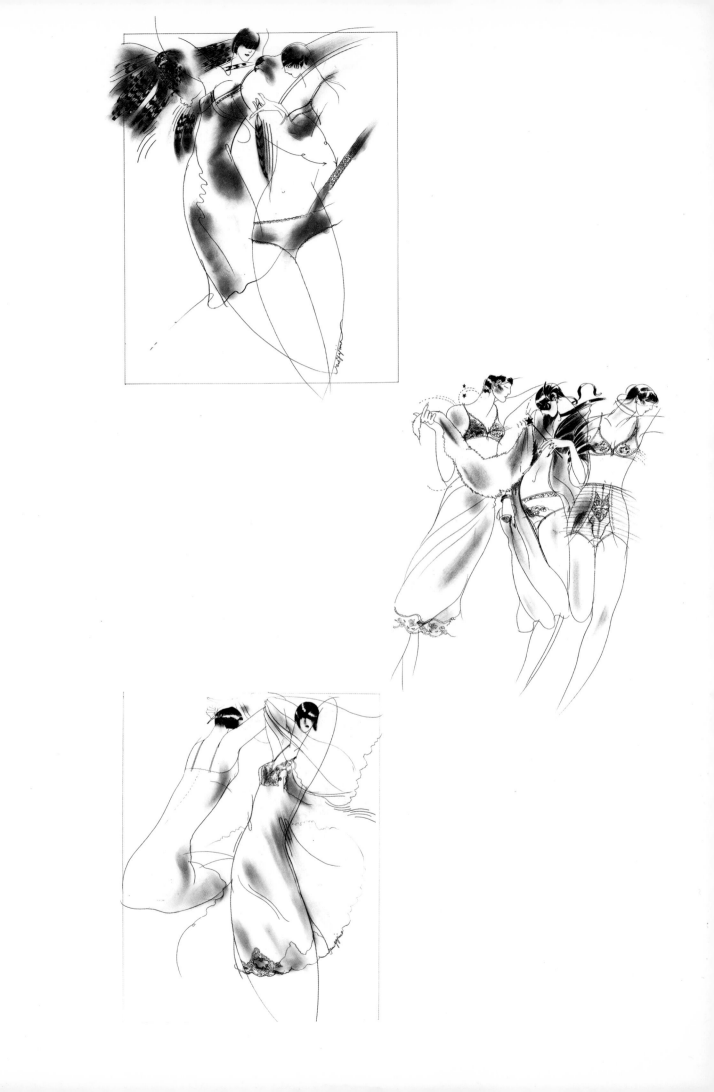

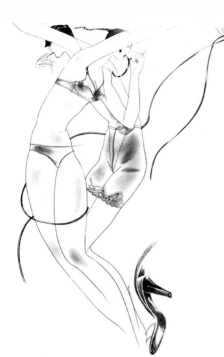

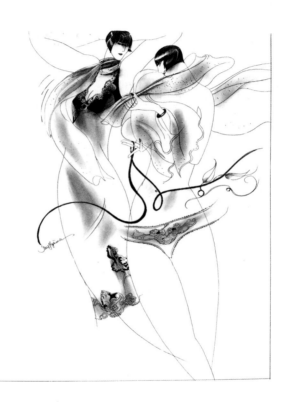

51.5 × 36.4 *Pencil, Pastel, Mat paper*

FIGURE DRAWING
FOR FASHION

花

風

23×18　*Pencil, Chinese ink, Drawing paper*

39.5×29.7　*Pencil, Skin paper*

43.5×31 Pencil, Chinese ink, Drawing paper

雨

43.5×31 *Pencil, Chinese ink, Drawing paper*

43.5×31 *Pencil, Gouache, Drawing paper*

39.5 × 29.7   *Pencil, Skin paper*

矢島功のモードイラストを一生描きつづけてほしい。"てらい"かもしれないが、ぼくは矢島功を「モードイラストレーションの射手」とよびたいのだ。

I hope Isao Yajima continues to make mode illustrations all his life. It may sound like affectation, but I would call Isao Yajima is the shooter of the mode of illustration.

(Copywriter)

平 野 健 作 （コピーライター）
Kensaku Hirano

彼のイラストは、10年以上にわたって描き続けているが、いまだにその魔力を失うことがない。何度見てもフレッシュな落ちつきがある。トレートは、あらゆるイラストのなかにさらにきわだった鮮度をもってイキイキとしている。矢島功のイラストは、まさに本誌のイラストの一つ「アイデンティティ」をもっている。

He has been doing illustrations for us for ten years or more and he never loses his freshness. He has a wonderful magical power. Isao Yajima's illustrations have identity.

(Chief Editor of Dansen magazine)

近 藤 恒 介　（Dansen編集長）
Kosuke Kondo

Kosuke Kondo

39 × 47   Pencil, Pastel, Mat paper

24.5 × 29　*Pencil Pastel, BB Kent paper*

40.5 × 28.2 *Pencil Conte, PM pad*

40.5 × 28.2 Pencil, Conte, PM pad

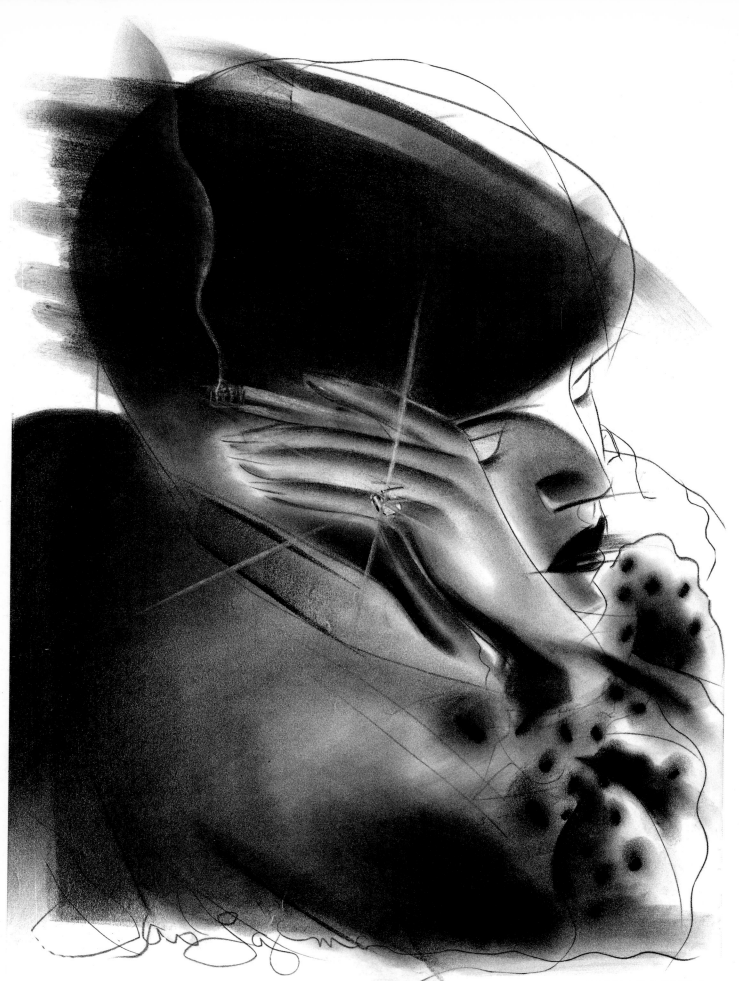

1982年8月の宝石たち

45×30 Pencil Pastel, Skin paper

人生は退屈のワルツ

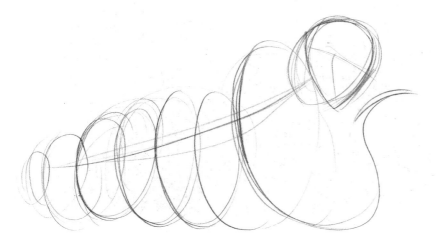

28.2×45   Pencil Pastel, Skin paper

32   *29.8 × 22.5   Pencil, Skin paper*

Illustration Isao Yajima

51.5×36.4 Pencil Watercolor, Fabriano paper

30.5 × 56 Pencil Airbrush (Gouache) Pastel, Fabriano paper

29.7 × 43   Pencil Skin paper

29.7×42 *Pencil Gouache, Kent paper*

36.4×25.7   Pencil, Gouache, Drawing paper

54.7 × 39.5   Pencil Colored pencil, Skin paper

37×29.7 Pencil Colored pencil, Skin paper

36.4 × 25.7   Pencil, Kent paper

36.4×25.7   Pencil, Kent paper

36.4×51.5   Pencil Watercolor, Fabriano paper

42×29.7   *Pencil Watercolor Marker, Skin paper*

36.4×25.7 Pencil Pastel, Kent paper

42×29.7   Pencil, Pastel, Skin paper

45

42 × 29.7   Pencil, Skin paper

46

36.4×25.7 Pencil Gouache, Watercolor paper

42×29.7 Pencil, Gouache, Fabriano paper

30 × 22   Pencil, Skin paper

42 × 29.7   Pencil Gouache, Fabriano paper

30 × 22   Pencil, Skin paper

42 × 29.7   Pencil Gouache, Fabriano paper

51

39.5×27.2 Pencil Gouache, Kent paper

29.5×22.8 Pencil, Skin paper

36.4×25.7　Pencil Gouache, KMK Kent paper

38.4×26.5　Pencil, Watercolor paper

42×29.7 Pencil Gouache, Kent paper 36.4×25.7 Pencil, Skin paper

56

TEATRO SCALA

42×29.5 Pencil Gouache, Kent paper

42 × 29.5   Pencil, Skin paper

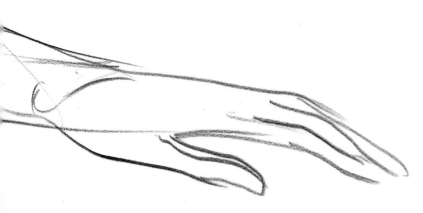

30×22   Pencil Watercolor, Kent paper
27.4×39.5   Pencil Gouache, Fabriano paper

40.5 × 28.2 Pencil Pastel, Skin paper

60

E sulla nave va il bianco e nero

Varata la nuova linea
«crociera» di Gianni Versace

47.8×33 Pencil Gouache, Fabriano paper

42 × 29.7   Pencil, Skin paper

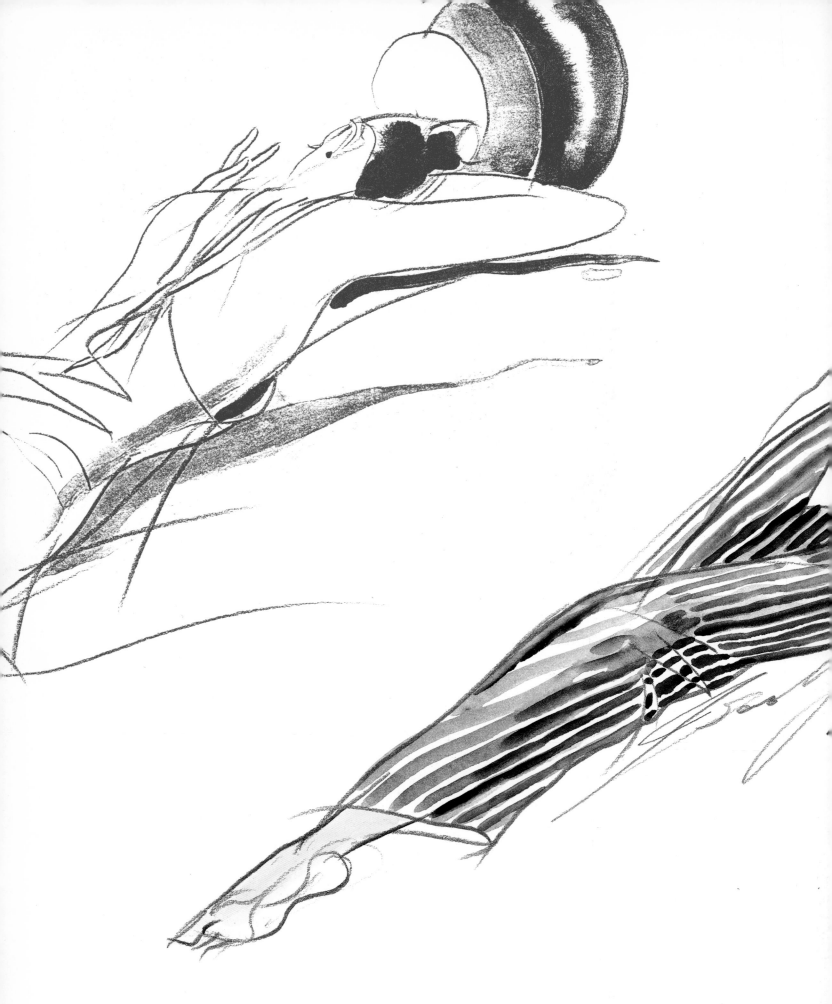

39.5 × 54.7 Pencil Watercolor, Fabriano paper

dorso: come
sensualissimo abito e
come complemento di
pantaloni rigati.

ATTUALITA' FLASH

Varata la nuova linea

29.7 × 42   Pencil, Skin paper

ATTUALITA' FLASH

Varata la nuova linea

Scollaturo vertigine sul dorso per l'abito lungo in seta.

39.5 × 27.3 Pencil Gouache, Kent paper
42 × 29.7 Pencil, Skin paper

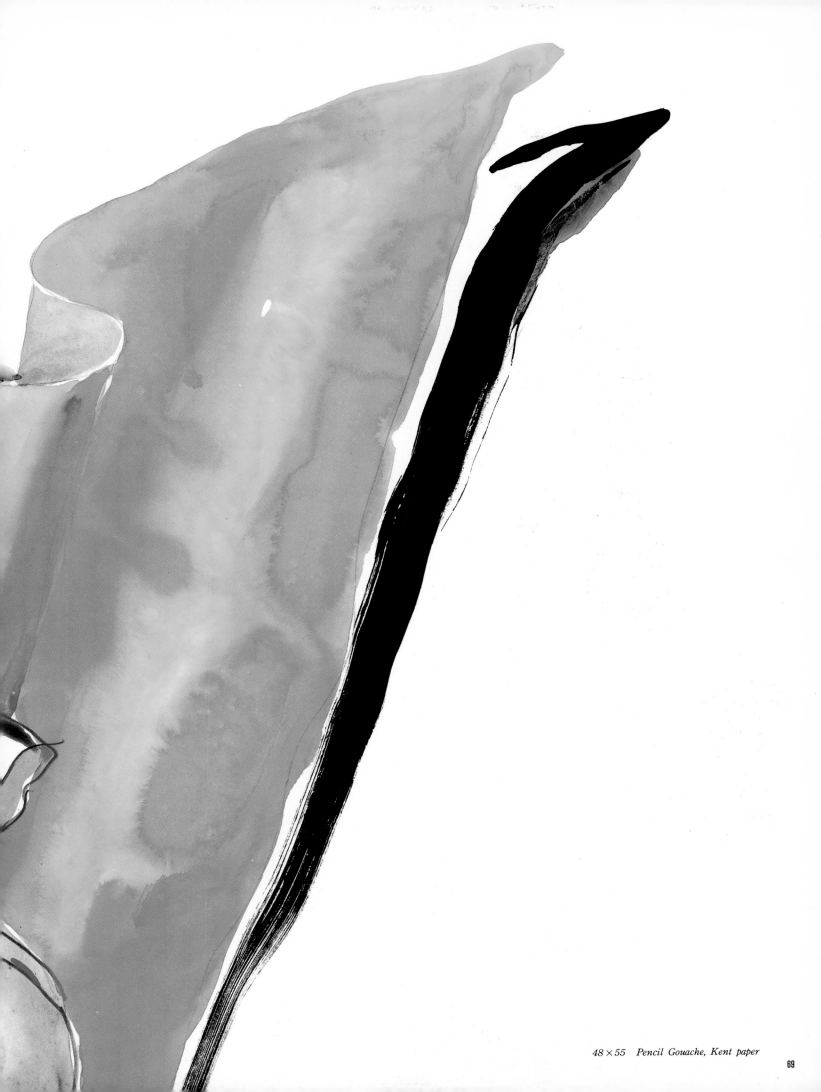

48 × 55 *Pencil Gouache, Kent paper*

42×29.7 *Pencil Gouache, Kent paper*

服は型押しでは出来ない、あらゆる部分に形をつくる仕掛けが秘められている。この丸みはどう仕立てられているのだろう、このフレヤーは、このドレープは、全体のラインは、とさまざまな面から体と布との関係を描いていく。

後ろの女は誰、こちらの男性は、どなた？　どんな人かしら？
………と、人物像を気にかけながら描く。

37.5×33.5 *Pencil Gouache, Watercolor paper*

42×29.7 Pencil Gouache, Fabriano paper

36.4×25.7 Pencil Gouache, Fabriano paper

こんな姿、君にもあるでしょう？　服の形や特徴だけを描くのも面白くない。

42×29.7　Pencil Gouache, Fabriano paper

42×29.7 Pencil, Gouache, Pastel, Drawing paper
36.4×25.7 Pencil, Watercolor, Fabriano paper

42×29.7 Pencil Watercolor, Kent paper

42×32.5 Pencil Gouache, Kent paper

38 × 23 Pencil Watercolor, Fabriano paper

39.5×31　Pencil Gouache Pastel,
Fabriano paper

42×29.7　Pencil Watercolor Colored pencil,
上質紙

38.5×32.5　Pencil Gouache, Fabriano paper

42×29.7　Pencil, Watercolor, Colored pencil,
Drawing paper

42×29.7 *Pencil Watercolor Pastel*, 上質紙

36.4×25.7 *Pencil Chinese ink Gouache, Watercolor paper*

42×29.7 *Pencil, Watercolor, Pastel, Drawing paper*

42×34 *Pencil Gouache, Kent paper*

42×31.5   Pencil, Skin paper

48 × 36   Pencil Gouache Colored pencil, Kent paper

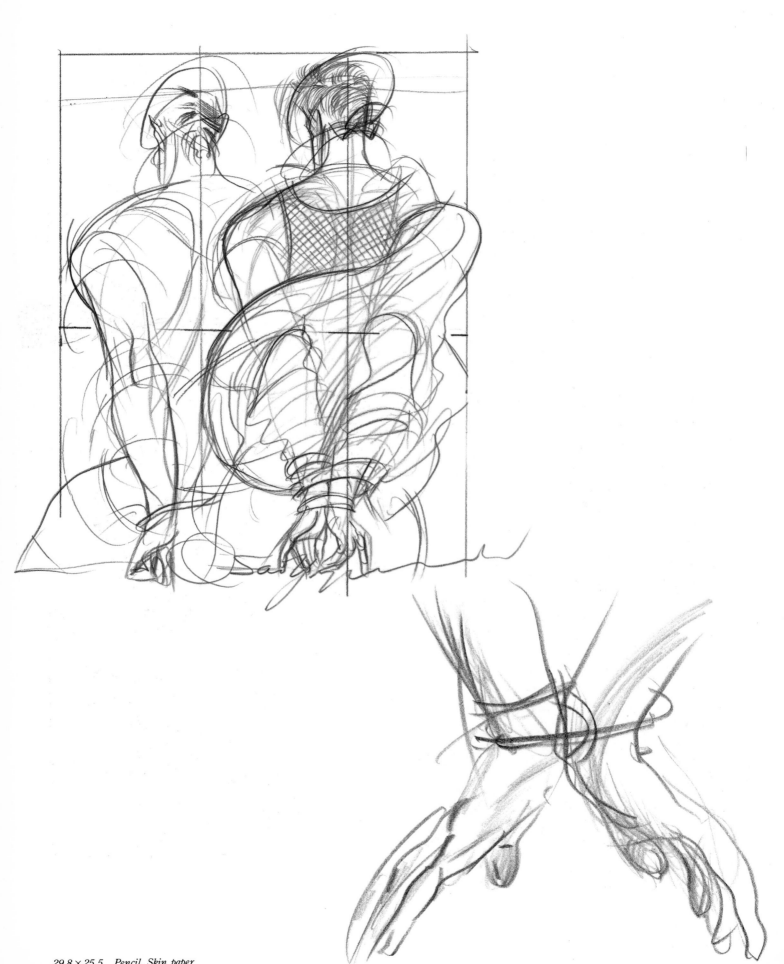

29.8 × 25.5   Pencil, Skin paper

39.8×31.2 Pencil, Watercolor, Colored pencil, Drawing paper

42×29.7 Pencil, Skin paper

illustrator
ISAO YAJIMA

illustrator
ISAO YAJIMA

42 × 29.7   Pencil, Skin paper

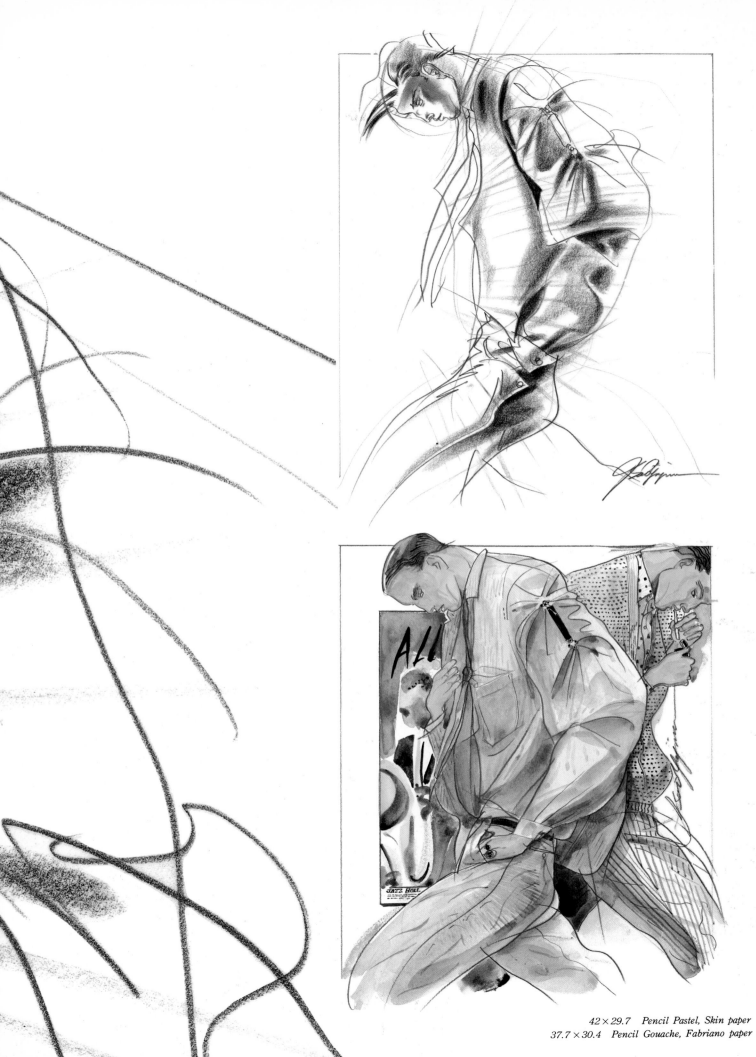

42 × 29.7   Pencil Pastel, Skin paper
37.7 × 30.4   Pencil Gouache, Fabriano paper

描き込みによって、服が多くを語り始めたら、顔は脇役で充分だ。

42×29.7 Pencil, Skin paper

40 × 29.5˙ Pencil Watercolor Conte Pastel, Kent paper

43.5 × 35.3   Pencil, Pastel, Colored pencil, PM pad

il settimanale della moda italiana
the italian fashion weekly magazine

pitti uomo a firenze, ventitreesima edizione
le collezioni di prêt-à-porter maschile e accessori
autunno-inverno '83-84
l'abbigliamento classico maschile e il suo rinnovamento:
ne parlano tessutai, stilisti, dettaglianti
gli stilisti a milano propongono
un uomo saggio, rustico... «povero»
le nuove cravatte invernali in un inserto a colori
pubblicità e nuove immagini dell'uomo sui mass-media

pitti uomo

42 × 29.7   Pencil Pastel Colored pencil, Skin paper

pitti uomo

COPIA NON IN VENDITA

il settimanale della moda italiana
the italian fashion weekly magazine

i dati economici di un mercato in ascesa
consumatori e dettaglio non accettano le stravaganze
gli stilisti e la pelle: un grande amore
per la pelle uomo anteprima primavera-estate '83
concia e confezione: viaggio in un mondo complesso
i divi del cinema e la virilità del cuoio

SETTIMANALE INDIPENDENTE PER L'INDUSTRIA IL COMMERCIO E LA MODA — GIORNALE TESSILE
ANNO XIII - N. 584 DEL 17 GIUGNO 1982 - SPEDIZ. IN ABB. POST. GR. II/70

l'uomo in pelle

ポーズは商品だ、とモデルは言う。ただの棒立ちでは商品は生きてこない。
数秒分の一の瞬間的な動きを与えることによって物語性が帯びてくる。

42×29.7 Conte pencil Pastel, Skin paper

l'uomo in pelle

42 × 29.7   Pencil Pastel, Skin paper

gT

il settimanale della moda italiana
the italian fashion weekly magazine

GIORNALE TESSILE
SETTIMANALE INDIPENDENTE PER L'INDUSTRIA IL COMMERCIO E LA MODA
ANNO XIV - N. 613 DEL 20 GENNAIO 1983 - SPED. IN ABB. POST. GR. II/70

undicesima edizione di pitti casual a firenze
idee, spunti, novità nelle collezioni autunno-inverno '83-84
**la situazione economica del settore nei pareri dei produttori
tra basic e moda d'avanguardia, dove va il casual?
in gruppo e in movimento le campagne pubblicitarie
prime anticipazioni dal sehm di parigi**

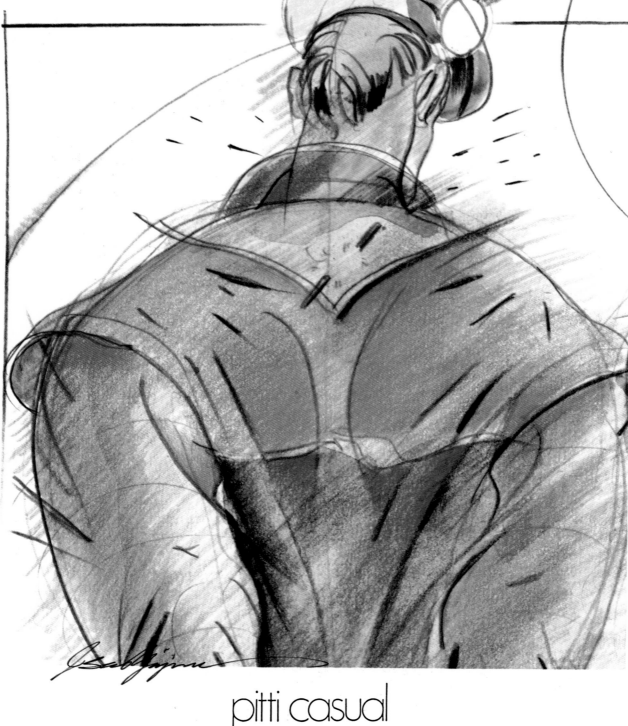

pitti casual

42×29.7   Conte pencil Watercolor Colored pencil, Fabriano paper

il settimanale della moda italiana
the italian fashion weekly magazine

pitti filati, undicesima edizione a firenze
la situazione economica del settore:
il mercato interno e quelli esteri in una nostra inchiesta
idee, spunti, novità per l'autunno-inverno '83-'84
comofoulard - proposte moda per l'estate '83
l'alta moda a roma e a parigi:
i sarti e le collezioni del prossimo inverno

GIORNALE TESSILE
SETTIMANALE INDIPENDENTE PER L'INDUSTRIA IL COMMERCIO E LA MODA
ANNO XIII - N. 594 DEL 9 SETTEMBRE 1982 - SPED. IN ABB. POST. GR. II/70

pitti filati

42 × 29.7   Conte pencil Colored pencil, Skin paper

42 × 35   *Pencil Watercolor, Fabriano paper*

PAL ZILERI ® by Forall - estratto da L'UOMO VOGUE

42×29.7 Pencil Pastel Watercolor, Fabriano paper

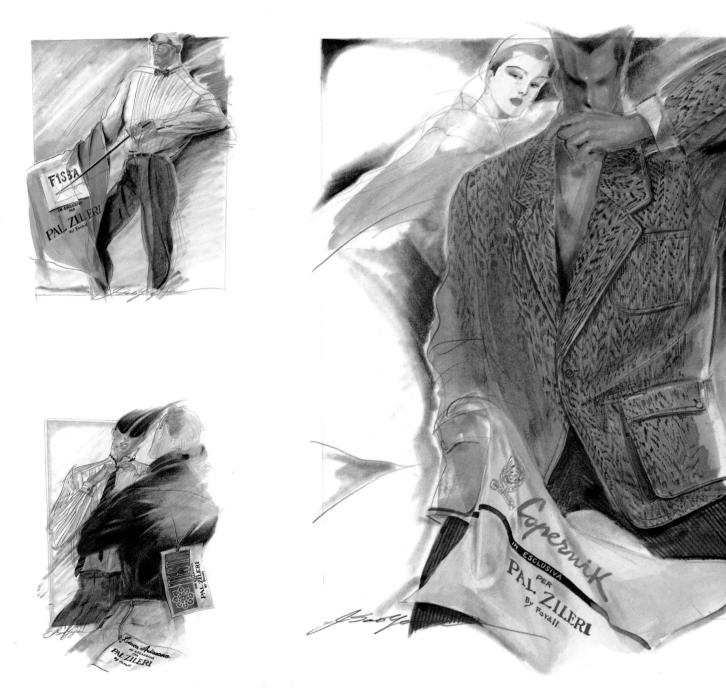

42 × 29.7   Pencil Pastel Watercolor, Fabriano paper

BOCCHESE GIUSEPPE E FIGLI
S.P.A. - VICENZA

gb seta
BOCCHESE
VICENZA - ITALIA

MODELLO
PAL ZILERI by FORALL

42 × 29.7   Pencil Pastel Watercolor, Fabriano paper

SO.DI.TEX
QUARONA SESIA (VC)

COORDINATO
PAL ZILERI by FORALL

42 × 29.7   Pencil Pastel Watercolor, Fabriano paper

KINGSLAND
CLASSICO

51.5 × 72.8   Pencil Pastel, Mat paper

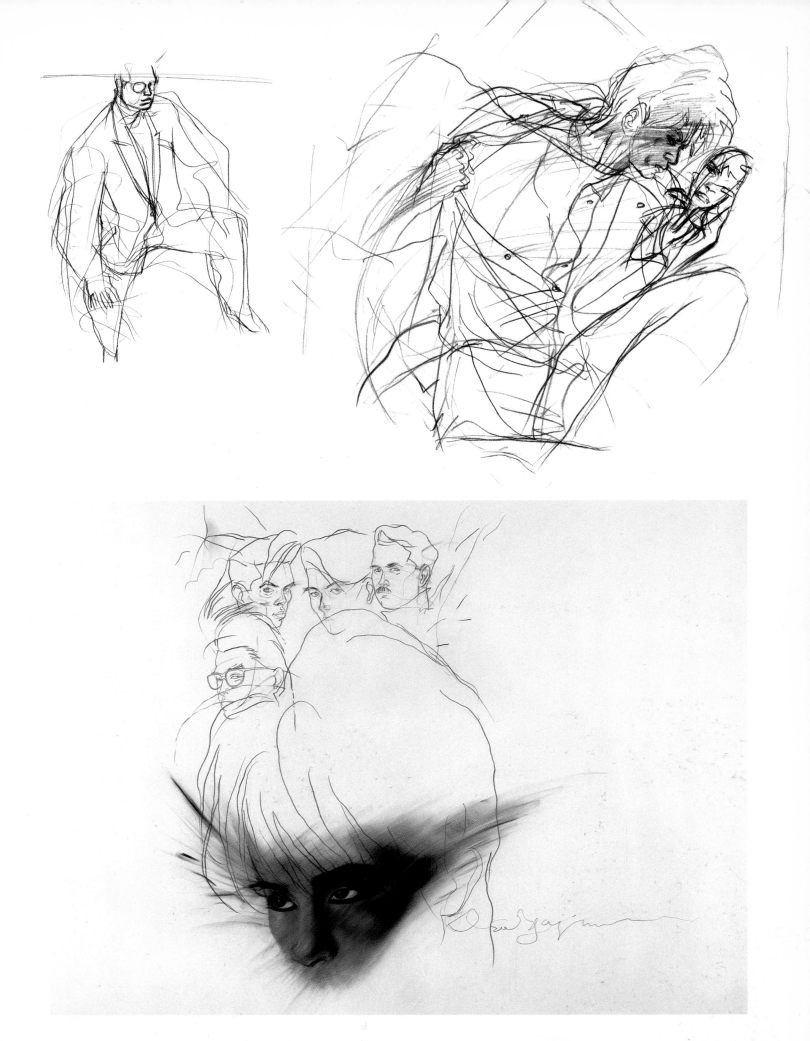

72.8 × 103   Pencil Pastel, Watercolor, Fabriano paper

FIGURE DRAWING FOR FASHION

FIGURE DRAWING FOR FASHION

42 × 31   Pencil, Pastel, Skin paper

72.8×51.5   Pencil Gouache Pastel, Fabriano paper

薄化粧。

37×28 *Pencil Gouache, Watercolor paper*

Wacoal

51.5 × 36.4 Pencil Gouache, Watercolor paper

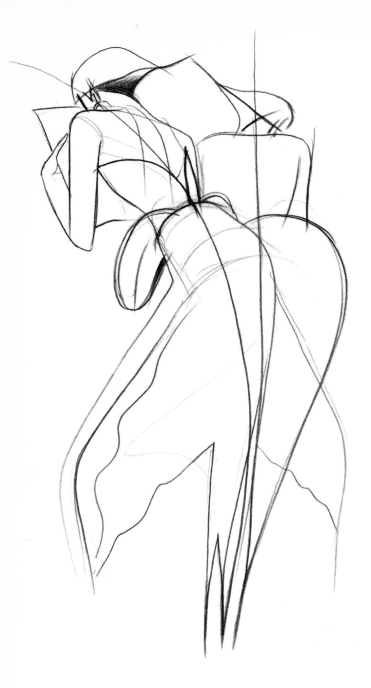

Orientation（順応）、
Concentration（集中）、
Purification（浄化）、
Absorption（没頭）、
Construction（構成）、
Destruction（破壊）、
Integration（統合）、
Actualization（実現）、
動きの速いものでも、
じっと、
観察しているうちに、
その姿が固定されているように、
次第に、
はっきりと見えてくる。

Orientation, Concentration, Purification, Absorption, Construction, Destruction, Integration, Actualization... even though moving rapidly, by observing for a long time and fixing the form you can gradually begin to sea clearly.

(Mode Illustrator)

矢島 功 （モードイラストレーター）
Isao Yajima

私は誰のものであるにせよ、素描に大変興味を持っている。それはモチーフに対し描き手の受ける最初の印象がそのまま単純な手法によって映し出され、再び描き直すことのできない生命感を帯び、加えて作者そのものの姿がそこに在るように感じるからである。

1979年、夏、ニューヨークのある美術館で、H・マチスの平面、立体の作品を大量に見たとき、今まで見てきた数点の作品から感じるマチス像がまったく違った印象で自分に飛び込んできた。私はその中で幾つかの素描を目にするうちに、知らずに筆跡を追従していた。それは簡素化されたマチエール、時に何度もチョークが走り、くり返えされ描かれていた。追従は途中から迷路に入り、ついに追い切れなかった……ことを覚えている。

素描の速度と間の追跡を通し、自分の速度を刺激させる。最近、ベニスにてエゴンシーレ、ミラノにてフランシス・ベーコンのそれを大量に見る。

31×19.5   Pencil, Pastel, PM pad

ISAO YAJIMA
1945 長野県生れ
1945: Born in Nagano Prefecture, Japan
1966 桑沢デザイン研究所卒業
1966: Graduated from the Kuwazawa Design Institute of Tokyo

PUBLICATION

WACOAL CO.,LTD.
FASHIONCOLOR (NIHON SHIKIKEN CO.,LTD.)
SOEN (BUNKA SHUPPAN)
ARGENT CO.,LTD.
25ANS (FUJINGAHO-SHA)
MAISON DE TOILE CO.,LTD.
GRUPPO ZANELLA (ITALY)
KASHIYAMA ITALIA (ITALY)
TOKYO LOOK
COPAN CO.,LTD.
ITALIAN VOGUE (ITALY)
DANSEN (STAIRU-SHA)
GT (EDIZIONI HENESSEN S.P.A)
MENS VOGUE
MONDOUOMO (ITALY)
MARUI CO.,LTD.
KITTY RECORD CO.,LTD.
MY CITY

ファッション ドローイング
Figure Drawing For Fashion

1986年8月25日 第1刷発行
August 25, 1986 First Publication
1990年5月25日 第6刷発行
May 25 1990 Sixth Publication
著者: 矢島 功(絵紗生)
Author: Isao Yajima
発行者: 久世 利郎
Responsible for Publication: Toshio Kuze
発行所: 株式会社グラフィック社
Publisher: Graphic-sha Publishing Company Limited
〒102東京都千代田区九段北1-9-12
1-9-12 Kudankita Chiyoda-Ku, Tokyo 102 Japan
Tel. 03-263-4318 Fax. 03-263-5297 振替・東京3-114345

印刷・製本：凸版印刷株式会社
Printing and Binding: Toppan Printing CO.,LTD.
写植：三和写真工芸株式会社
Typesetting: Sanwa Shashin Kogei CO.,LTD.

編集協力：アトリエKO
Planning, Layout, and Editing; ATORIE KO CO.,LTD.
東京都渋谷区神南1-5-14三船マンション703
703 Mifune Mansion 1-5-14, Jinnan, Shibuya-Ku, Tokyo, Japan.
Tel. 03-464-8936 Fax. 03-770-3465

ISBN4-7661-0389-0 C3071

オトコとか、オンナとかの姿にこだわりを持たないことからファッションにもう一つの顔が生れる。キミがかつてオトコだった時、オンナだった時をそれぞれ想い出せばよい。

il settimanale della moda italiana · the italian fashion weekly magazine

COPIA L. 3500

GT - GIORNALE TESSILE - ANNO XVI - N. 712 - 8 GENNAIO 1985 - SPED. IN ABB. POST. GR. II/70 -

fashion

UOMOMODA

THE OFFICIAL PRESENTATION
OF ITALIAN MENSWEAR COLLECTIONS